M is for Mayflower

A Massachusetts Alphabet

Written by Margot Theis Raven
Illustrated by Jeannie Brett

Sleeping Bear Press
310 North Main Street
P.O. Box 20
Chelsea, MI 48118
www.sleepingbearpress.com

Printed and bound in Canada.

10 9 8 7 6 5 4 3 2 1

Library of Congress Cataloging-in-Publication Data

Raven, Margot Theis.
M is for Mayflower: a Massachusetts alphabet / written by
Margot Theis Raven; illustrated by Jeannie Brett.
p. cm.
Summary: Presents information about the state of Massachusetts
in an alphabetical arrangement.
ISBN 1-58536-072-4
1. Massachusetts—Juvenile literature. 2. English
language—Alphabet—Juvenile literature. [1. Massachusetts. 2.
Alphabet.] I. Brett, Jeannie, ill. II. Title.
F64.3 .R38 2002
974.4—dc21

Aa

Our beginning letter **A**
starts this book a special way,
for A stands for Algonquin (AL-GONE-QWIN),
the native language of the tribe
that gave our state the name
which fills us all with pride —
Massachusetts!

The Algonquian language, spoken by the Massachuset tribe of Native Americans, gave our state its name which means "large hill place." The name refers to Great Blue Hill, the tallest (rising 635 feet) of the 22-hill Blue Hills chain found near Boston. Residents of Massachusetts were also officially designated Bay Staters on December 18, 1990. This name comes from the Pilgrims' first settlement on Cape Cod Bay.

Massachusetts is a small state, the 45th largest in the United States, but it has a widely varied topography. Its land ranges from rocky beaches along its coast, to fertile valleys and rivers in its central sections, to the Berkshire Hills mountain range in the western half of the state. Mt. Greylock in the Berkshires rises 3,491 feet, making it the state's highest spot.

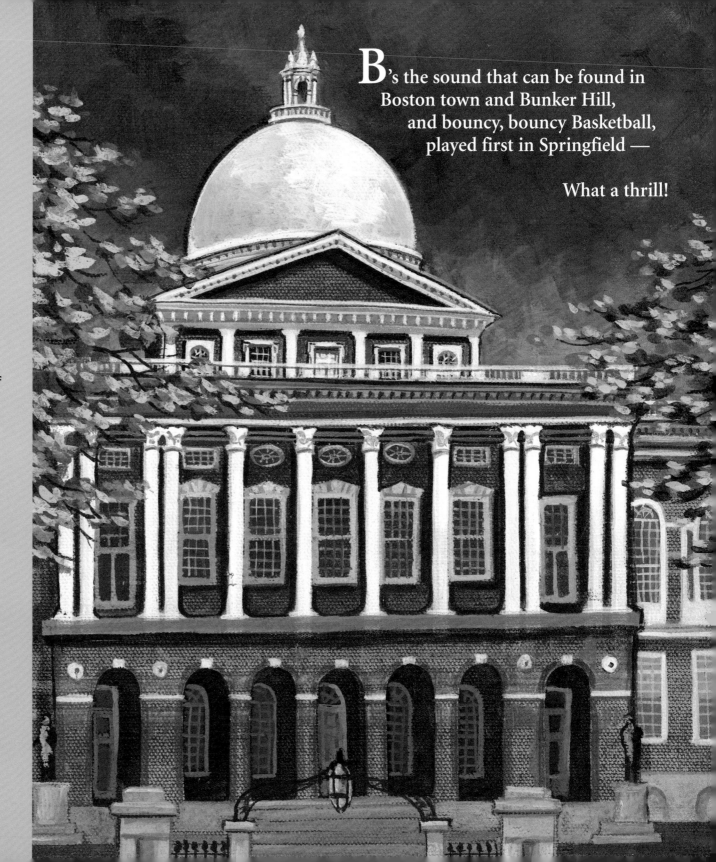

Boston, the state's capital, is a busy seaport and the largest city in New England. Boston got its name in 1632 from the English Puritans who founded the city on the peninsula and made it the capital of the Massachusetts Bay Colony. The Puritans called Boston after their hometown in England.

Because they thought that cooking on Sunday was a sin, the Puritans often made baked beans on Saturday to eat as Sunday dinner, earning Boston the nickname, Beantown.

Outside Boston is Bunker Hill, the site where the first major Revolutionary War battle was fought.

Springfield is the site of the first game of basketball. It was invented by Dr. James Naismith, a physical education teacher, in 1891 using peach baskets for hoops.

Bb

B's the sound that can be found in
Boston town and Bunker Hill,
and bouncy, bouncy Basketball,
played first in Springfield —

What a thrill!

Used from early days as food and fertilizer, the cod is olive gray in color and weighs from ten to twenty pounds. Its image has been featured on stamps, coins, and official seals. The Sacred Cod, a five-foot-long wooden fish carved in 1784, hangs in the Massachusetts House of Representatives' Chamber. It points north when Democrats hold the majority, and south when Republicans do so.

Massachusetts grows more than half of America's cranberry crop. Used to make cranberry juice, jams, and jellies, the tart berry grows on the South Shore coast, and is native to Plymouth, the Islands of Nantucket, and Cape Cod.

Each fall, the ripened, red berries turn wetland bogs into beautiful pools of brilliant crimson. In Massachusetts you will find more than 12,000 acres of cranberry bogs!

C is for Cod which swim in the sea,
and Cranberry bogs as red as can be.
Both are state symbols, rich in history!

D is for Duckling — hurry, make way!
They parade in the Public Garden all day.
And D is for Duck Tours that drive on the street,
then splash in the river — bring your webbed feet!

Dd

As the first botanical garden in the country, Boston's Public Garden has hundreds of trees of 74 species. Each spring it colorfully bursts forth with thousands of newly planted tulip bulbs.

In the Garden are two of Boston's most loved attractions: the pedal-powered Swan Boats, operated on the lagoon since 1877; and the bronze statuettes of Mrs. Mallard and her eight little ducklings, characters from the 1940 Robert McCloskey classic children's book, *Make Way for Ducklings*.

Other Boston sights can be seen from the high vantage of World War II amphibious vehicles operated by the popular Boston Duck Tours. The steel tubs first drive through Boston neighborhoods such as Back Bay, then the tubs head straight into the Charles River, for a SPLASHingly good cruise along the Esplanade.

Now we've come to the letter E.
It's the American Elm, our state tree.
In spring and summer its leaves are green —
but they're golden-yellow when fall foliage is seen.

E e

The American elm was named our state tree in 1941. It received the honor because in Cambridge, July 3, 1775, General George Washington stood beneath the great elm when he took charge of the Continental Army. Sadly, the tree is no longer there. Since 1930, Dutch elm disease has stricken the American elm and its species, resulting in a widespread loss of beautiful trees.

The prime "leaf peeping" road in Massachusetts is known as the Mohawk Trail. Opened in 1914 as New England's first scenic road, it was once an old Pocumtuck and Mohawk Indian footpath.

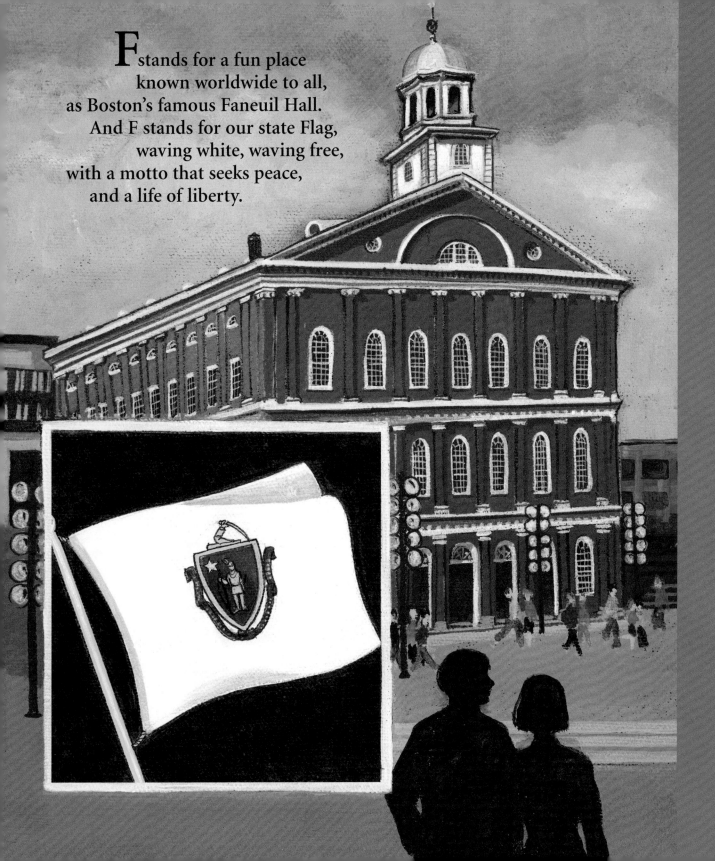

F stands for a fun place
known worldwide to all,
as Boston's famous Faneuil Hall.
And F stands for our state Flag,
waving white, waving free,
with a motto that seeks peace,
and a life of liberty.

Given to Boston in 1742 by Peter Faneuil, Faneuil Hall was once a market. The building houses the meeting hall called the "Cradle of Liberty," where patriots like Samuel Adams once made impassioned speeches for freedom.

Behind Faneuil Hall is Quincy Market which features fun shops, restaurants, jugglers, balloon-blowing clowns, musicians, comedians, flower vendors, food and ice cream vendors galore!

Our state flag bears the coat of arms of the Commonwealth on both its sides; however, until 1971, the flag had a pine tree on one of its sides. The blue shield shows: a Native American holding an arrow pointed downward in peace; a star depicting Massachusetts as one of the original 13 colonies; and a sword with our motto "By the sword we seek peace, but peace only under liberty."

Ff

F

THEY THAT GO
DOWN TO THE SEA
IN SHIPS

G is for Gloucester.
Watch whales in the ocean.
They jump and they leap
like sea-fountains in motion.

G g

In the 1700s, the whaling industry boomed as whales were harpooned for profit near fishing towns such as New Bedford, Provincetown, and the Island of Nantucket. People used the whales' oil to light lamps in America and Europe. Whale by-products were used to make candles, corset stays, and perfume. When kerosene and petroleum were discovered in the 1800s, the whaling industry died off. Whale killing is now banned, but whale watching is a favorite pastime.

Founded in 1623 and the oldest fishing port in the United States, Gloucester is a whale-watching town. Narrated whale cruises leave from the wharves. Visitors can also see the famous Fishermen's Memorial, Man at the Wheel, which is dedicated to the fishermen "that go down to the sea in ships."

H h

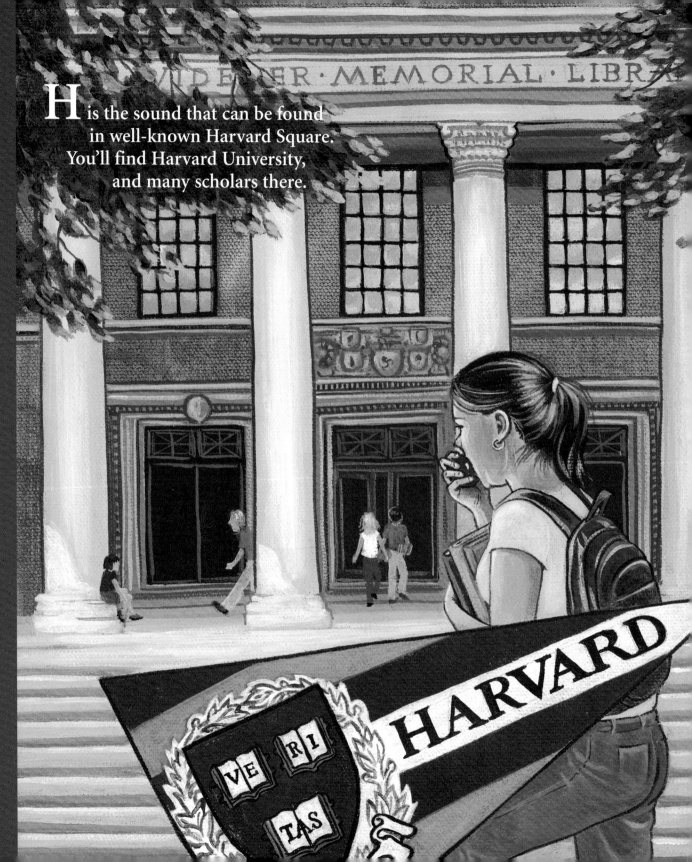

H is the sound that can be found
in well-known Harvard Square.
You'll find Harvard University,
and many scholars there.

Harvard Square is actually a triangle. It is home to Harvard University, but it has many fun stores and shops around it, too. Harvard University is located in the city of Cambridge. Harvard was the first college in America, established in 1636. Famous Harvard students include: seven U.S. presidents and nearly forty Nobel laureates.

Today, Harvard is one of many public and private colleges and universities located in Massachusetts. Others include: the University of Massachusetts, Amherst College, Emerson College, Boston College, Boston University, and Mount Holyoke College.

The islands off Massachusetts — Martha's Vineyard, Nantucket, curved-armed Cape Cod, the Elizabeth Islands, and the Boston Harbor Islands — were formed by glaciers more than 10,000 years ago. In the 1700 and 1800s, the islands' rocky cliffs and bays made hideaway havens for the roving pirate bands traveling the Atlantic Ocean. Legends abound about buried treasures still not found.

Today, as well as being havens for protected wildlife and plant species, the islands are known as busy, popular vacation places where thousands of visitors and tourists arrive each summer to enjoy days in the sun and nights eating lobsters and clams — seafood treasures!

I is for Islands
where pirates hid treasure,
    but forgot where they put it;
oh, they should have known better!

Finders keepers, losers weepers!

CAPE COD BAY

CAPE COD

BUZZARD'S BAY

ELIZABETH ISLANDS

NANTUCKET SOUND

MARTHA'S VINEYARD

NANTUCKET ISLAND

ATLANTIC OCEAN

I i

Julia Ward Howe, an ardent abolitionist during the time of slavery, lived at 13 Chestnut Street in Boston's Beacon Hill neighborhood. During the Civil War, Julia visited a Union Army camp and became inspired to write the poem, Battle Hymn of the Republic. Published in 1862 in *The Atlantic Monthly* and later set to music, it quickly became a popular song during the Civil War. Howe's house is located on Boston's Women's Heritage Trail, a historical walking route highlighting the lives of famous Massachusetts women.

Boston's Black Heritage Trail honors its African-American community, including their service in the Massachusetts 54th Regiment. It was the first Black regiment from the North to fight in the Civil War.

J j

J is for Julia—
    Julia Ward Howe.
She wrote a great battle hymn
    that still is sung now.

K k

In 1848 when Patrick Kennedy arrived in Boston from Ireland, he had no idea that his great-grandson, John Fitzgerald Kennedy, would some day become the youngest president of the United States.

John's father, Joseph P. Kennedy, married Rose Fitzgerald, the daughter of a Boston mayor. Joseph dreamt that his children would go into politics, too. His dream was fulfilled when JFK was elected president in 1960, but the dream didn't last long; after just three years in office, John Fitzgerald Kennedy was assassinated.

In Boston you can visit the JFK Library, the JFK Museum, and the Brookline house where JFK was born.

Three other United States presidents came from Massachusetts: John Adams, John Quincy Adams, and George Herbert Walker Bush.

Now **K** stands for JFK—
That's John F. Kennedy.
He was our 35th president
and died in 1963.

Now turn the page
for the letter L,
with a Revolutionary
story to tell...

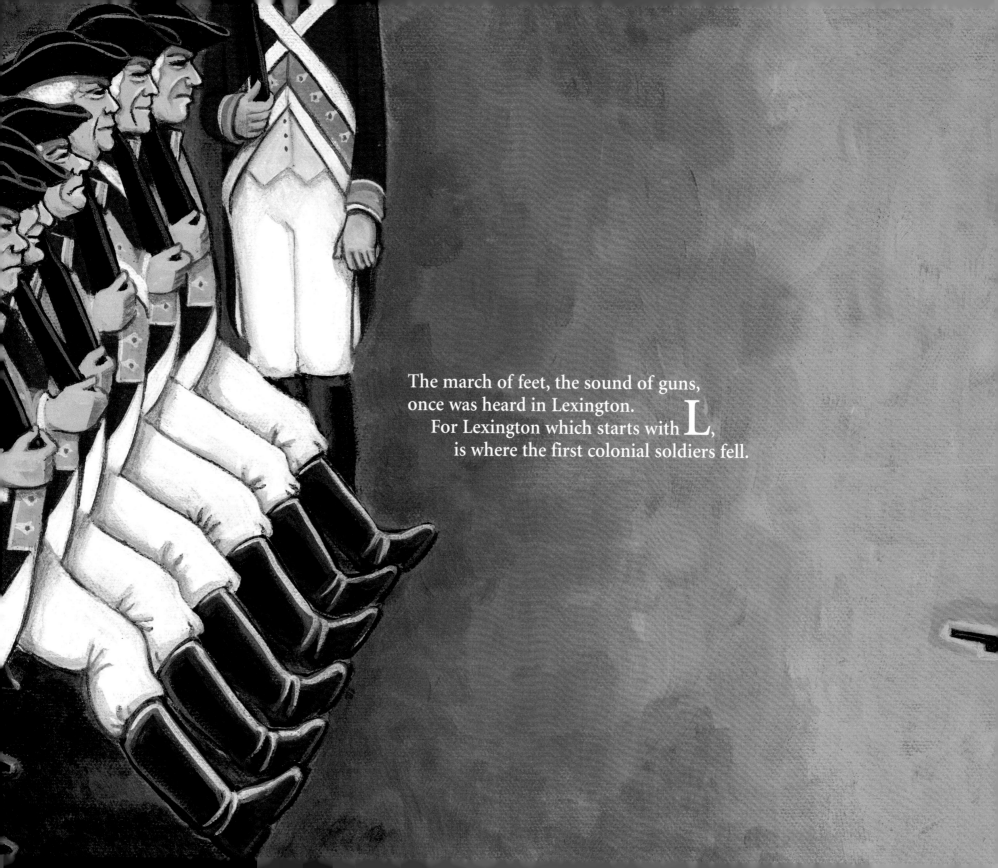

The march of feet, the sound of guns,
once was heard in Lexington.
   For Lexington which starts with L,
      is where the first colonial soldiers fell.

The first skirmish for American freedom occurred in the village of Lexington on the morning of April 19, 1775.

After having marched through the night en route to the town of Concord to seize the colonists' hidden weapons, British soldiers (redcoats) stopped in Lexington. Suddenly, at the village green, 77 minutemen (the colonists' army of citizen-farmers who pledged to be ready to fight in one minute) met the redcoats. Cries were heard and shots were fired.

When the noise stopped, eight minutemen lay dead as the British moved on to Concord. At Concord's Old North Bridge, the colonial militia now fired at the redcoats, killing several of them. The war for independence had begun.

Ll

Before carrying 102 Pilgrims from England to Plymouth, Massachusetts, the 180-ton *Mayflower* sailing ship transported tar, lumber, wine, and spices in the Mediterranean.

The Pilgrims set sail on September 6, 1620, seeking religious freedom. Their 66-day voyage ended when they landed on Cape Cod. They anchored at Provincetown on November 11 where they signed the Mayflower Compact. On December 6, a scouting party found Plymouth Harbor, and on December 16, the *Mayflower* arrived, as legend says, at Plymouth Rock.

During the first winter at Plimoth Plantation, half of the Pilgrims died, but friendly Wamponoag Indians helped the remaining settlers survive. In thanks, the Pilgrims invited the Indians to a harvest feast in November 1621.

The mayflower is also our state flower. It has fragrant white and pink flowers that bloom in the spring.

m
M

It was long ago, from far away
    when our letter M sailed here one day.
Fueled by wind and faith's great power,
M carried Pilgrims and the name Mayflower.

Born in New York City in 1894, Norman Rockwell moved with his family to Stockbridge, Massachusetts, in 1953. He lived and painted there until his death at the age of 84 on November 8, 1978.

In 1916 at the age of 22, Rockwell painted his first cover for the weekly magazine, *The Saturday Evening Post.* More than 300 covers followed over the next 47 years. His artful images celebrated the humor, warmth, and innocence of the American people. Rockwell also painted portraits of U.S. presidents Eisenhower, Kennedy, and Johnson, and various world leaders.

Rockwell's studio and art are now preserved in Stockbridge in the Norman Rockwell Museum.

With a paint brush in his hand,
the letter N's a famous man,
who was known from coast to coast,
as an illustrator for *The Saturaday Evening Post*.
Can you guess his name? Should we tell?
Our N, of course, is Norman Rockwell!

Old North Church, also called Christ Church, was built in 1723. It is immortalized by Henry Wadsworth Longfellow's poem about Paul Revere's ride to warn the colonists that, "the British are coming!"

While much praise is given to Revere, it was daring church sexton Robert Newman who, on April 18, 1775, made the dangerous climb on a tall ladder up the darkened church steeple with the two signal lanterns.

On his ride Paul Revere, a silversmith by trade, was actually joined by two other brave horsemen: William Dawes and Samuel Prescott. Only Prescott made it all the way to Concord. All three men were caught, but Prescott got away to sound the alarm, "through every Middlesex village and farm."

O is for Old North Church.
In its steeple two lanterns were hung,
so Paul Revere could warn the people,
the war with Britain had begun!

Emily Dickinson was a poet,
and poet starts with P,
but shy Emily wrote poems for herself,
not for others to see.

P p

Born in 1830 in the college town of Amherst, Emily Dickinson was terribly shy and spent most of her 56 years in a brick house built by her grandfather. After her father died in 1874, Emily rarely left her house. She took to dressing all in white in her later years.

Emily began to write when she was twenty, but most of her poetry was written between 1858 and 1865. After Emily's death in 1886, her sister found nearly 1,800 poems in her room. They were bound together in 40 sewn books. While only ten of her poems were published during her lifetime, Emily Dickinson is known as one of our most respected poets.

Our state bird is the black-capped chickadee. Known also as the titmouse and dickybird, its song is always a happy one: chick-adee-dee-dee!

"Water, water everywhere,
but not a drop to drink,"
until the Quabbin Reservoir
brought it to the sink!
See what a **Q** can do for you?

In Massachusetts' Pioneer Valley, the 55,000-acre Quabbin Reservoir provides drinking water to Greater Boston. It is one of the largest man-made public water suppliers in the United States and was created by the construction of two earthen dams.

In 1939, the four towns in the Swift River Valley were flooded to make the reservoir. All of the inhabitants of the four towns were moved from their homes. Their houses and business were torn down or relocated. At Quabbin Park Cemetery rest the graves that were also relocated from the flooded towns.

Eighteen miles long, the reservoir holds 412 billion gallons of water when full and supports 27 species of fish.

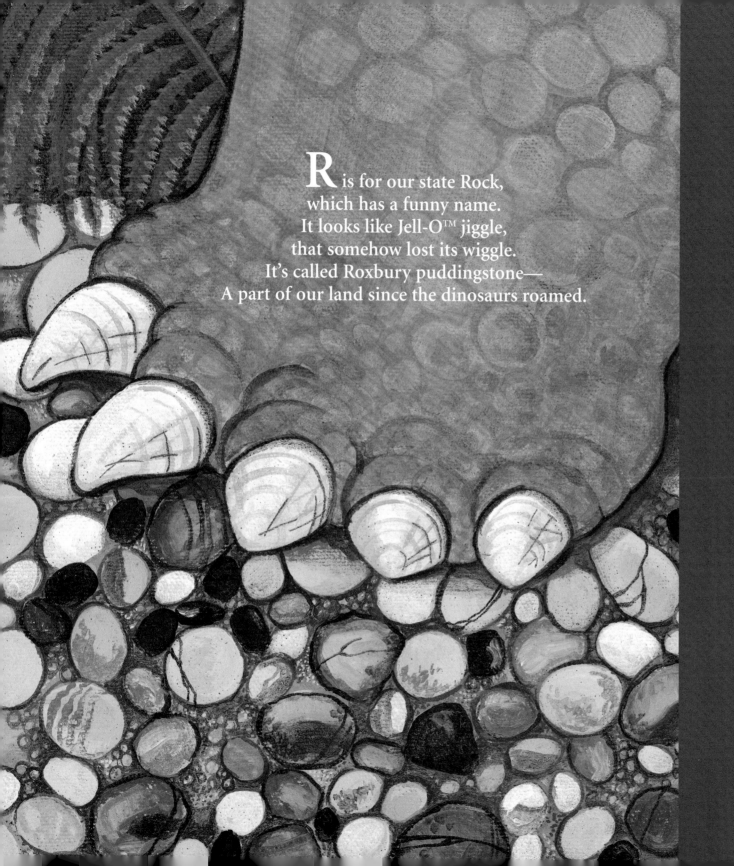

R is for our state Rock,
which has a funny name.
It looks like Jell-O™ jiggle,
that somehow lost its wiggle.
It's called Roxbury puddingstone—
A part of our land since the dinosaurs roamed.

The Roxbury puddingstone became the state rock in 1983. It is also called the Roxbury conglomerate because it was formed out of debris swept up by glaciers — bumpy pebbles, rocks, clay, and sand. Cleaned by the ocean and sandwiched for millions of years under boulders, the glacier deposits were eventually cemented together by the forces of heat and pressure.

Many old churches in Boston are built out of puddingstone. A descendant of Paul Revere even sent a 30-ton puddingstone boulder with a bronze memorial plaque on it to the Civil War battle site of Gettysburg, Pennsylvania, in 1886.

R r

Now **S** is for Salem
on Halloween night
when kids dress as witches —
a fun, frightful sight!

Originally established as a fishing settlement in 1623, Salem is rich in Revolutionary War history. Its many historic sites include the Peabody Essex Museum, the Salem Maritime National Historic Site, and the House of the Seven Gables.

Salem is also steeped in literary connections. It is the birthplace of American novelist Nathaniel Hawthorne, best remembered for his novels *The Scarlet Letter* and *The House of Seven Gables*, the latter tale said to be inspired by the original house.

Salem may be best known for its 1692 Witch Trials when villagers accused each other of practicing witchcraft. More than 100 people were said to be witches and imprisoned. In time, the people of Salem realized their charges were false and the trials stopped. Today, for spooky fun on Halloween nights, many visitors line up to tour Salem's Witch House where the judge of the trials once lived.

After the Tea Act of 1773, the colonists staged the Boston Tea Party as a sign to England that they would not pay heavy taxes on tea. Samuel Adams gathered together his "Sons of Liberty" to dress as Indians and throw 342 chests of British tea into the Boston Harbor. The British responded by closing the port of Boston and passing more punishing laws.

For more than 60 years, the Berkshires have been a training center for musicians and the summer home of the Boston Symphony Orchestra at Tanglewood. Each season, between late June and Labor Day, more than 300,000 visitors come to enjoy concerts at the open-sided Music Shed and on the rolling lawn.

Here's a little T for two,
and a two for T —
They are: the famous Boston Tea Party
and Tanglewood's Boston Symphony.

For 20 years Elis Stenman constructed his two-room house in Pigeon Cove out of 100,000 sheets of newspaper, as an experiment after inventing a special paste. The walls are 215 sheets thick and are lacquered on the outside, and the furniture is made of rolled-up newspaper!

Once an old trolley bridge, the Bridge of Flowers in Shelburne Falls spans the Deerfield River. More than 500 species, including bulbs in the spring, bloom on both sides of the lovely walking bridge.

Blackstone River Valley's Lake Chargoggagoggmanchaugagoggchaubunagungamaug has the longest name of any lake in the country. It is now called Webster Lake for short. Its original Nipmuc Indian name means: "You fish on your side of the lake, I fish on my side, and no one fishes in the middle."

U is for the Unusual places
you can find around our state—
a Paper House, a Bridge of Flowers,
and a lake with a name you can pronounce for hours.
Want to give it a try?
It's Lake Chargoggagoggmanchaugagoggchaubunagungamaug!
Oh, my!

U u

If you visit Old Sturbridge Village
you will find that the letter **V**
stands for a town from yesteryear—
a place to learn your history.

Old Sturbridge Village, near the Connecticut state border, is a restored, mid-nineteenth century period village on 200 acres. Presenting the daily life of a small New England town from 1790 to 1840, it was founded by three brothers, Channing, Albert, and J. Cheney Wells, whose hobby was collecting American primitive antiques. Purchasing an old farm that included a sawmill, gristmill, and millpond, the brothers and their grown children collected other historic buildings from villages throughout New England to create a living village.

In 1946, Old Sturbridge Village opened with 81 visitors. Today, more than half a million visitors annually enter houses, shops, and even walk over an old covered bridge to go back in time.

On July 4, 1845, Concord writer and resident Henry David Thoreau went to live alone in a 10- by 15-foot house near a pond in some woods. Thoreau went there because, as he later wrote, he wished to live simply and wisely.

In all, Thoreau spent two years and two months at Walden Pond. His book, *Walden: or Life in the Woods*, published in 1854, related his studies of nature while there. Today, a large pile of rocks sits beside the spot where his house once stood. People write their names on the rocks and sometimes a message.

Concord had many famous writers at that time including: Nathaniel Hawthorne, Ralph Waldo Emerson, and Louisa May Alcott, author of *Little Women*. These celebrated literary figures are buried near one another on Author's Ridge in Sleepy Hollow Cemetery.

Now **W** stands for the peaceful pond,
that Henry David Thoreau lived on.
It's called Walden and it can be found
in historic, lovely Concord town.

All over the islands of Nantucket, Cape Cod, and Martha's Vineyard are windmills and lighthouses, the surviving examples of some of the oldest structures of these kinds in America.

Built in 1745, the Old Mill on Nantucket is the oldest, still functioning windmill in the country. It stands over 50 feet high, with four blades 30 feet in length, and is called a smock-type of windmill, from the early agricultural costume it resembles.

The Eastham Windmill, built in Plymouth in 1680, is the oldest windmill on Cape Cod.

Cape Cod's first lighthouse stands in the town of Truro. Still working today, it is an 80-foot tower called Highland Light. First lit by whale oil lamps, it stood watch over the waters in 1797. The original lamps were used until the turn of the twentieth century.

X

X

When Nantucket's windmills turn around, X they make dancing X's on the ground.
Do you see the X? X? X?
You bet! bet! bet!

Yy

Now Y is the shape
the rivers' forks make
as they branch and flow
and roll through our state.

Massachusetts has 4,230 miles of flowing waters and over 1,100 lakes and ponds. Its largest river is the Connecticut, with approximately 100 miles of it running through the state. At twenty-five miles broad at its widest, the Connecticut River flows south from Vermont and into Connecticut passing through Massachusetts' beautiful countryside.

Surprisingly, Massachusetts also gets more rainfall across the state — 43.8 inches per year — than "rainy Seattle" in the Pacific Northwest, which gets over 37 inches annually.

So many rivers, so little time…
isn't that a silly rhyme?
On the next page, find one more…

As the first elected Postmaster General of the Colonies, Boston-born Benjamin Franklin would have been pleased that patriotic Sudbury received the zip code of 01776—America's year of Independence!

Zip codes began on July 1, 1963, when a five-digit code was assigned to every address in the country by the U.S. Postal Service. The first digit showed a geographical area, from zero in the Northeast to nine in the West. The next two digits pinpointed population and common transportation areas. The last two digits pinpointed small post offices or zones near large cities. Sudbury received the coveted 01776 zip code when it, and other historic towns nearby, were given their numbers in alphabetical order.

Sudbury, incorporated in 1639, is one of the oldest towns in New England, and is the site of the famous Wayside Inn where Henry Wadsworth Longfellow was inspired to write of Paul Revere's midnight ride.

A zero, a one, two sevens and a six—
are some patriotic numbers that you can mix.
A Massachusetts' Zip code Z
(zip code starts with Z)
is 0-1-7-7-6, for old Sudbury!

Now, you've read from A to Z
of the many wonderful things to see
in our great state, the place to be!
Massachusetts—the birthplace of liberty!

A Boatful of Massachusetts Fun Facts

1. Massachusetts has the oldest working Constitution in the world. It was ratified in 1780, nine years before the Constitution of the United States! What is the native language of the oldest residents of Massachusetts?

2. Massachusetts is a state but it is also called a Commonwealth, because the term is contained in its Constitution. It means a whole body of people, but in the 1700s, the term also meant republic. The states of Kentucky, Pennsylvania, and Virginia are also Commonwealths. How and when did the people of Massachusetts come to be called Bay Staters?

3. Massachusetts became a state on February 6, 1788. In size what does it rank among other states in the union?

4. Patriot John Hancock was governor when the state seal was adopted on December 13, 1780. What human figure is depicted on the seal's blue shield? Hint: you can see it on the flag! What does the figure hold and why?

5. Until 1971, one side of the state flag had a tree on it instead of the state seal. What kind of tree was it?

6. What is the motto written on the state seal's coat of arms?

7. Massachusetts' ten largest cities are: Boston; Worcester; Springfield; Lowell; Cambridge; Brockton; New Bedford; Fall River; Lynn; and Quincy. What national sports game was first played in one of these cities? Which city was it?

8. In which of these cities was the oldest college in America founded? Why was it established?

9. What is Massachusetts' state flower? Hint: it is also the name of a ship that transported tar and lumber before people.

10. How many days did the Pilgrims' voyage on the *Mayflower* last after setting sail from England on September 6, 1620?

Answers

1. Algonquian
2. The name became official on Dec. 18, 1990. It originated from the Pilgrims' first settlement on Cape Cod Bay.
3. 45th largest
4. An Indian holding an arrow pointed downward as a sign of peace.
5. A pine tree
6. "By the sword we seek peace, but peace only under liberty."
7. Basketball was played first in Springfield.
8. Harvard University was established by the Puritan clergy to educate future ministers.
9. The *Mayflower*
10. 66 days

Reference List

Andres, Alan & Bell, Brian. 2000. *Insight Guide Boston.* London: APA Publications.

Booth, Robert. 2000. *Boston's Freedom Trail.* Guilford, CT: The Globe Pequot Press.

Braun, Ester K. & Davie P. 1994. *The First People of the Northeast.* Lincoln, MA: Moccasin Hill Press.

Davis, William J. 1996. *Massachusetts Wildlife Viewing Guide.* Helena and Billings, Montana: Falcon Press Publishing Co.

Freeman, Stan & Nasuti, Mike. 1998. *The Natural History of Eastern Massachusetts.* Florence, MA: Hampshire House Publishing Co.

Holmes, Robert. 2000. *Passport's Illustrated Guide to Boston & New England.* Chicago, Illinois: Thomas Cook, Passport Books.

Jameson, W.C. 1998. *Buried Treasures of New England.* Little Rock, Arkansas: August House, Inc.

Locke, Tim & Gordon, Sue. 2001. *Fodor's Exploring Boston & New England.* New York: Fodor's Travel Publications.

Masoff, Joy. 2000. *American Revolution 1700-1800.* New York: Scholastic Inc.

Masoff, Joy. 2000. *Colonial Times 1600-1700.* New York: Scholastic Inc.

Mc Allister, Jim. 2000. *Salem, from Naumkeag to Witch City.* Beverly, MA: Commonwealth Editions.

McGovern, Loretta. 1998. *Boston, The Official Guidebook to Boston and its Neighborhoods Including The Freedom Trail.* Boston, MA: Parsons, Friedmann & Central, Inc.

Moore, Alex W. Jr. 1996. *Concord Authors, Biographical Notes.* Concord, MA: Anaxagoras Publications.

Perk, Jeff. 1998. *Massachusetts Handbook.* Emeryville, CA: Avalon Travel Publishing Inc.

Rogers Radcliffe, Barbara & Rogers, Stillman. 1999. *Massachusetts Off the Beaten Path.* Old Saybrook, CT: The Globe Peguot Press.

Warner, J. F. 2000. *Massachusetts.* Minneapolis, MN: Lerner Publications Co.

Margot Theis Raven

Margot Theis Raven has been a professional writer working in the fields of radio, television, magazines, newspapers, and children's books for thirty years. She has won five national awards, including an IRA Teacher's Choice award. Margot earned her degree in English from Rosemont College and attended Villanova University for theater study, and Kent State University for German language. Margot has: four children; Scott, Bryan, Michael, and Ashley; a wonderful husband, Greg; and three dogs. She splits her time living in Concord, MA, Charleston, SC, and West Chesterfield, NH. *M is for Mayflower* is her second children's book with Sleeping Bear Press. She also authored *Mercedes and the Chocolate Pilot: A True Story of the Berlin Airlift and the Candy that Dropped from the Sky*, illustrated by Gijsbert van Frankenhuyzen.

Jeannie Brett

Jeannie Brett grew up in the coastal town of Hingham, Massachusetts, where she developed a passion for animals and the outdoors that continues today. Jeannie studied at the School of the Museum of Fine Arts in Boston and at the Minneapolis College of Art and Design. Jeannie lives in York, Maine, with her husband, Greg, and their three children, Gregory, Sophie, and Lee. They share their home with two horses, two bunnies, three enormous cats, and a wonderful old Newfoundland. *M is for Mayflower* is her second children's book with Sleeping Bear Press. She is the illustrator of *L is for Lobster: A Maine Alphabet*.